WHOEVER YOU ARE

WHOEVER YOU ARE

By MEM FOX   Illustrated by LESLIE STAUB

SCHOLASTIC INC.

New York Toronto London Auckland Sydney
Mexico City New Delhi Hong Kong

ISBN 0-590-20027-5

Text copyright © 1997 by Mem Fox.
Illustrations copyright © 1997 by Leslie Staub.
All rights reserved.
Published by Scholastic Inc., 555 Broadway, New York, NY 10012,
by arrangement with Harcourt Brace & Company.
SCHOLASTIC and associated logos are trademarks and/or registered trademarks of Scholastic Inc.

12 11 10 9 8 7 6 5 4 3   9/9 0 1 2 3 4/0

Printed in the U.S.A.   14

First Scholastic printing, January 1999

The illustrations in this book were done in oil on gessoed paper.
The hand-carved frames were made from
plaster, wood, and faux gems.
The display type was hand-lettered by Judythe Sieck.
The text type was set in Monotype Goudy Bold
by Harcourt Brace & Company Photocomposition Center,
San Diego, California.
Color separations by Bright Arts, Ltd., Singapore
Printed and bound by Tien Wah Press, Singapore
This book was printed on totally chlorine-free Nymolla Matte Art paper.
Production supervision by Stanley Redfern and Ginger Boyer
Designed by Judythe Sieck

For Hanan Ashrawi
—M. F.

For YaYa
and for you,
whoever you are
—L. S.

Little one,
whoever you are,

wherever you are,

there are little ones
just like you
all over the world.

Their skin may be
different from yours,
and their homes may be
different from yours.

Their schools may be
different from yours,

and their lands may be
different from yours.

Their lives may be
different from yours,

But inside,
their hearts are
just like yours,

whoever they are,
wherever they are,
all over the world.

Their smiles are like yours,

and they laugh just like you.

Their hurts are like yours,
and they cry like you, too,

whoever they are,
wherever they are,
all over the world.

Little one,
when you are older
and when you are grown,

and they may be different,
wherever you are,
wherever they are,
in this big, wide world.

But remember this:

Joys are the same,
and love is the same.

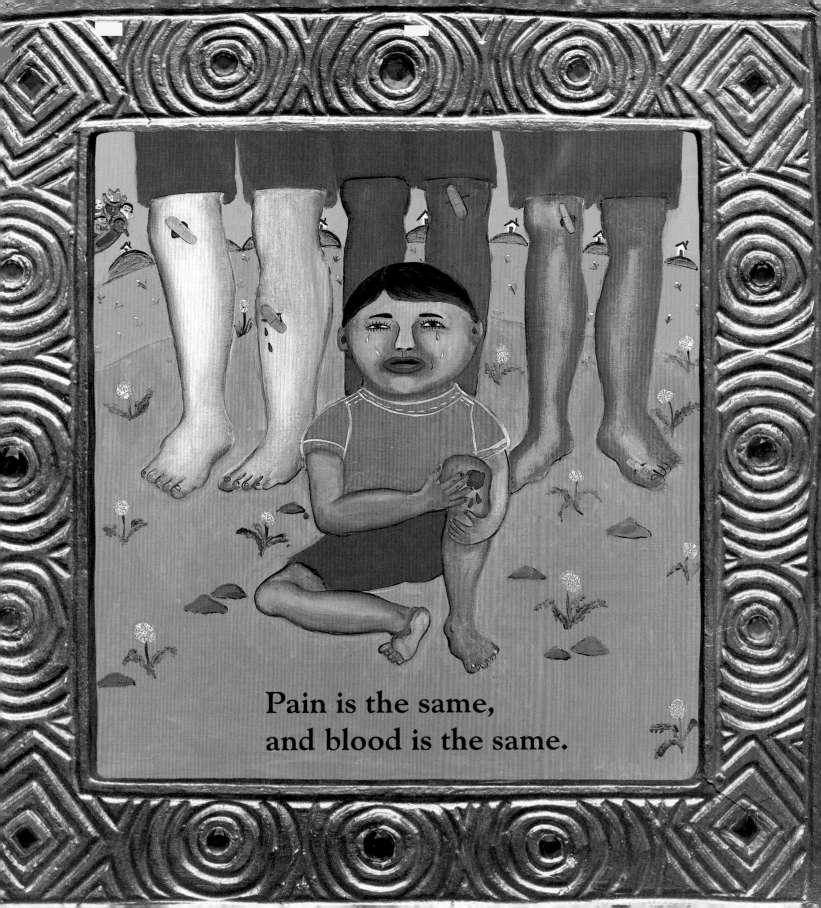

Pain is the same,
and blood is the same.

Smiles are the same,
and hearts are just the same—
wherever they are,
wherever you are,
wherever we are,

all over the world.